FOREWORD

It's 1981, year of the Royal Wedding, and punk is still in. A group of friends hang out and Daz arrives late to join them. What follows is the unfolding of Daz's story as he seeks refuge in the false warmth of the drugs' embrace. Dealing with issues around drug misuse and broken families, *Dragon Chaser* charts Daz's nervous breakdown and interaction with characters in a psychiatric unit, before he emerges on the other side.

The play offers scope for the use and imaginative development of physical theatre skills. In addition to the main, character-based cast, there is a chorus (for a flexible number of performers) who act as both inner and outer commentators. The chorus perform as an ensemble in a tightly choreographed, physically and vocally inventive group. The language used aims to juxtapose lyricism and poetry with the darkness of the experiences being portrayed. It uses references to fairy tales as a structuring device to move the text away from graphic realism to something more mythical.

Dragon Chaser requires a minimum cast of 9 (with doubling). However, it is intended for a much larger group: up to 35, with a large chorus. Scene divisions make it ideal for use during lessons or youth theatre sessions and the chorus scenes are suitable for group exploration and devising.

Plays with Attitude have been written to appeal to teenage performers and audiences. They are also designed to offer a text-based framework for developing the individual and ensemble physical performance skills explored by students through class-based improvisation. *Dragon Chaser* is suitable for Sixth Form or capable Key Stage 4 (aged 15+).

CAST LIST

Gang members

DAZ BRIGHTSON	Dresses as a punk
JEFF	Dealer
ROSY	
MINNIE	
ADE	
COL	
BEL	Daz's girlfriend

TEACHER
MOTHER

Psychiatric Unit

DOCTOR GEOFF
NURSE ROSE
AMEENA
AIDEN
COLIN
BELLADONNA

CHORUS   Ten are specified, but can use variable numbers. Used for narration, commentary, visual effect and creating physical backdrop to scenes.

Clothes are colour-coded to tell Gang and Unit members apart.

Set requirements – two or three short, light benches and a series of stools. Rugs and material throws optional.

DI AVO

DE

&

ser

HODDER
Wayland

For Vera Anna Fusek Peters

British Library Cataloguing in Publication Data

Peters, Andrew, 1962-
Dragon chaser. - (Plays with Attitude)
1. Drug abuse 2. Children's plays, English
I. Title II. Peters, Polly
822.9'14

ISBN 0 7502 3728 7

Printed in Hong Kong by Wing King Tong

Hodder Children's Books
A division of Hodder Headline Limited
338 Euston Road, London NW1 3BH

ACT 1

Blackout. Moving spotlight shows skateboarder (DAZ) *skating across stage left to right. Lights up: shabby living room.* JEFF *is asleep on sofa (bench). Gang watch TV.*

CHORUS can either be physical theatre props depending on cast size, or figures arranged as a tableau frieze of wallpaper at back of stage throughout this scene. TV in corner is created physically by performers with NEWSREADER *seated behind.*

NEWSREADER: Today on the 29th July 1981, over 700 million viewers around the world saw the Prince of Wales and Lady Diana Spencer getting married at St Paul's… And the crowd are cheering as they ride to Buckingham Palace in a horse-drawn carriage, Prince Charles in his Naval uniform, and Lady Diana, the former kindergarten helper in a confection of billowing ivory silk with puffed sleeves. It was, said Robert Runcie, the Archbishop of Canterbury, 'the stuff of which fairy tales are made'.

CHORUS cheers. There are shouts of We love you Lady Di, Atta girl, Bonnie Prince Charlie, Big Ears has Landed, *etc.* NEWSREADER *fades to a mumble.*

MINNIE: Isn't that sweet, what a lovely couple! Don't you think so, my darling lemon-Ade? [*Sarcastic*]

ADE: [*Looking up from book*] What, Brainless and Big Ears? You must be joking.

5

ROSY: [*Looking round from mimed mirror*] Minnie's right. It's a love story. Give 'em a chance. Any excuse to get dressed up. I think it's romantic…

COL: It's a fairy tale. Fair enough? Fairy nuff! [*All groan*]

ALL: Nice one Colin,

          Nice one son,

          Nice one Colin,

          Let's have another one!

JEFF *groans, wakes up.*

MINNIE: [*Looks at* JEFF] All right, Jeff? You look like a corpse.

JEFF: [*Groans again*] Yeah, dead cool. Too much blow.

ADE: Too much doesn't exist in your vocabulary, our dear divine dealer man. Got any gear?

JEFF: Yeah, yeah, yeah. Just let me wake up will you?

ROSY: [*Excited*] Come on Jeff, we're supposed to be partying. Tonight is the night to celebrate!

MINNIE: Can't wait!

JEFF: Minnie Ha-Ha-Ha? Don't know about that. This opiated black will do your head in! [*Giggles*]

MINNIE: Such a honeymoon high! [*Swirls of silk. Dramatic*]

ADE: Milk and honey.

COL: Talkin' of nosh, I've got the munchies!

ROSY: Out to lunchies!

COL: We'll serve up a feast of funk and punk on tap.

ADE: Party time for the prince and his lady to die for. Lady to Di for. Lady Di. Geddit?

All groan.

ROSY: Where's Daz then?

COL: Probably duffing up a few skinheads.

JEFF: Or puffing after skinning up.

ADE: Never know with Daz.

MINNIE: Wouldn't want to meet him in a dark alley. In fact a
           dark alley wouldn't want to meet him in a dark alley.

ROSY: Give him a break. He's not like that.

MINNIE: What, hard? Put it this way, this guy has a sister
           called Cement.

ROSY: Not surprising, considering what happened to him.

JEFF: Yeah, yeah, yeah. Hey, d'ya think that Prince
           Whatsisface Charlie gets off his face on charlie?

*All fall backwards simultaneously, laughing, crawl to back of
stage, freeze.*

DAZ *spotlit centre stage, positioned as if he is a marionette.
The words of the* CHORUS *cue his specific set movements.*

CHORUS: Here is Daz at the start of the day – upright!
           [DAZ *jerks up*]
           Here is Daz at the end of the day – out of sight!
           [*Slumps to floor*]
           In between, hard but shy [*Hand on mouth*]
           Prefers to get high [*Looks up*]
           Likes to party [*Dances*]
           Lives in the corner [*Squats*]
           Smoking [*Mimes*]
           Snorting [*Mimes*]

7

Drinking [*Mimes*]

Man with the stuff!

Two from CHORUS *peel off and approach* DAZ *with false smiles*

So nice to see you!

1:        Instant friends [*Arms round* DAZ]

2:        It's never enough.

3:        Tripping [DAZ *trips*] No, *tripping* you fool.

DAZ: Ah!

4:        Take a tab:

Chorus begin synchronised tick-tock rhythm.

GROUP 1: Tick-tock

GROUP 2: Tickety-tock

GROUP 3: Tick-tack-tock

As rhythm builds, DAZ *moves to each sound spaced out.*

Rhythm accelerates, stops suddenly.

5:        Puking.

6:        Lurching home.

7:        Paranoid about police.

8:        Found in charge of a bicycle under the influence.

9:        One more before bed

10:       La-la land

1:        But it's never enough, so let's do it again.

Movements speed up this time.

1:        Shy

2:        High

3:        Toke

4:        Snort

5:      Trip

6:      Puke

7:      Lurch

8:      Home

9:      Bed.

DAZ *is on bench now as* CHORUS *circle him.*

1:      Over and over

2:      Night in, night out

3:      The merry-go-round of de-nial

4:      A river in Egypt!

5:      Just a bit of this.

6:      Just a bit of that.

7:      No needles, so it's all right, all right?

8:      You have to ask why

9:      He likes to get high?

10:     Don'tcha be so nosy

1:      Let's just say, everything in the family garden

2:      Is not so rosy.

Cut back to gang, getting ready for party.

JEFF: [*Hunched over table skinning up a joint*] Rosy! Shut
        that door! Can't have my blow blowing about all
        over the place.

Gang come to life in party mood. Early eighties music. CHORUS
repositioned as wallpaper

JEFF: Where were we, then?

ROSY: Party time, party time!

ADE: Celebrate that wedding!

COL: With lager, draw,

ADE: And more and more

MINNIE: Skinning up and spacing out.

COL: Speaking of space cadets, it's Orbit Man!

DAZ *enters, wearing big red wig with tiny Union Jack sticking out of it.*

COL: Love the wig, Daz! [*All chant, friendly*] Ear wig go,
             ear wig go, ear wig go…

JEFF: All right, Dazzler? [*Quieter*] Got my stuff? Up to
             speed? I trust you.

DAZ *nods.* BEL *slips on stage, sits on sofa. She looks up at* DAZ,
who is silently going round greeting everyone. Eyes meet, JEFF
introduces them: Bel, Daz. Daz, Bel. DAZ *doesn't say much, but
he's all right. Music gets louder.* BEL *moves to other side of
room but stares at* DAZ. *All improvise party scene. Sirens from
offstage. Followed by sounds of windows breaking, police
sirens, doors smashing.*

COLIN: Here's trouble. Scary, scary, scary… [*Spaced out*]

ROSY: It's a bust!

ADE: [*Pushing out chest*] It's a huge bust!!!

ROSY: Oh please, Ade, give us a break! We need to move it.

JEFF: [*Shouts*] Flush it all down the loo! Eat the evidence!

MINNIE: Yes, please. Mmmmm.

ROSY: This is no joke, Minnie. My mum will kill me. Back window – now!

ALL: Ear wig go! Ear wig go! Ear wig go!

Everyone tumbles offstage. Gang vanish, leaving DAZ *and* BEL *sauntering down street miming beginning to talk and have fun.* CHORUS *come forward.*

1:   Bel meets boy, meets lust.

2:   Romantic scene?

3:   No.

4:   Drugs bust.

5:   Bel chats,

6:   Boy dreams,

7:   Sirens sing in the soundscape of city screams.

8:   She doesn't laugh,

9:   Thinks he's not half

10:   Bad.

1:   They go for a toke

2:   And a joke

3:   Easy talk as they walk the river of streets and dawdle by neon pools.

4:   But crucial,

5:   The crux,

6:   She doesn't understand.

7:   For him, it'll only be a

ALL: One night stand.

Music as DAZ *and* BEL *improvise further mimed action. Music fades.*

Spotlight on BEL.

BEL: It was the wig that got me. A curly wig on a hard man. I had to laugh. And then the bust and that crazy running through the streets. Out of breath, keys in the door and tumbling up stairs trying to keep quiet and something about his mum on sleeping pills, don't worry, you know. What with the lines on the mirror and all the speed numbing our noses, one minute we were gabbling like demented geese and the next it was no demure kiss and 'Get your number, good night, what are you doing tomorrow?' His hands had a life of their own, all over me. It was a rush through and through. Daz might be a hard man, but that soft mouth of his could kiss all my troubles away. Don't get me wrong, I'm no slag. I let him go so far. Then stopped. I had to get home. Suddenly, he was embarrassed. Something in him just shut down. A lot of mumbling, scrawled phone numbers. He was still stoned. God knows if he would get to school the next day. Jeff tells me he's like this all the time. Something to do with family. He really was out of it… I mean, I do a bit, have a good time at the weekend, but every day? Well, what's to worry, eh…? We arranged to meet the next evening and now I'm waiting. And waiting… Maybe that's him ringing now.

Ringing sound. BEL *exits.*

DAZ *enters centre stage to phone box (mimed with bodies as props, a hand as phone).* DAZ *dials, with choral ringing tone sound effects from* CHORUS.

1:	Who's he gonna ring?
2:	The girl who finds she fancies this bloke?
3:	Or
4:	My Lord of Pills, Thrills, Smoke and Toke?
5:	Love's too soft a soppy healer
6:	Cut it out and
ALL:	Ring the dealer!

Ringing tone stops. DAZ *mumbles into phone – don't hear the actual words.*

7:	These drugs, make a cover-up jobby
8:	On speed he goes completely gobby
9:	Let's just say his dad—

Character steps out and perform exaggerated marionette mime of DAZ's *dad's story.*

10:	Was a little bit sad.
ALL:	Ahhhhhh!
1:	Not drugs,
2:	But a lack of hugs
3:	Stuck on depression's out-of-date shelf,
4:	Topped himself.
5:	Story with a gory ending.
6:	With dadless Daz pretending
6:	He cares not a jot
7:	Better to blot it out

8:        With a pogo-ing punk

ALL: Oi, oi, oi!

9:        Shove and shout.

Punk music blares on. CHORUS *transform into punks, pogo-ing up and down.* DAZ *stands in the middle, silent and still. Music fades and pogo-ing continues silently as we hear his voice.*

DAZ: I dress in studs and spiky hair, all black, all leather, all chains. I have perfect punk etiquette and stare at people in the street until they look away. I spit as I stalk past to let them know who's king of this coked-up castle. That Bel, that beautiful Bel got too close for comfort. Who believes in Happy Ever After anyway? Tonight, I am hard and the cracks are glued together. I know the music here, know all the words off by heart. We give each other hand signals, know the code. Bottle of amyl does the rounds. I snort and my heart goes turbo. I think I'm going to die, but don't. I'm alive for another thirty seconds. Lager is sticky on my boots, glue sticky in my nose. There's a fog of fag above our heads and this… this is togetherness. These are my mates. And my brother? Never got over our mad dad doing what he did. Poor brother, with his needles and pale skin and eyes pinned and gouching out, and falling asleep with a fag in his mouth. One day he won't wake up, I tell you. My mother has enough on her plate to worry about him. I'm just a nibbler, a side dish, nothing like him. Just a bit of the natural herbal, a few white powders. I'm not the problem… With my gang we wallow in tube trains, pick old fag ends off the floor and roll new ones. Squeeze glue into plastic bags and hear the tongues in our head. I am on fire now.

I dance. I am the lord of the dance.

Music stops.

All freeze then lurch against each other, miming pushing on to bus (with shouts of Single please, Child return, Honest I'm only six, What bum fluff? *etc.) while arranging benches appropriately. They sit, facing audience,* DAZ *in middle. All lurch left, then right simultaneously and bob and lean in time to rhythm of driving.* DAZ *looks sick.*

1:        [*Singing*] The eyes in my head go

ALL: Round and round, round and round, round and round!

2:        The kids on the bus are

ALL: Off their face

3:        All night long!

1:        This man is an artist of chuck!

2:        Out of the back of the bus.

3:        His stomach mixes up the palette from his palate

4:        His mouth is the spray can

All lurch left and make sounds of vomiting.

5:        It's not art as we know it, Jim.

6:        What goes down must

7:        Come up!

8:        And the streets are his canvas:

9:        Every mile

10:       Covered in his colourful bile...

1:        He is the

2:        Sultan of Sick!

3:        Viceroy of Vomit!

6:        Duke of Puke!

4:        Overdosed and feeling shitty

5:        Intimate of toilet bowls throughout the city!

All stand, stagger off bus. CHORUS *walk together with* DAZ *in the middle as if* CHORUS *are one entity, staggering from side to side, fumbling with key.* MOTHER, *standing in single spot, confronts* CHORUS *and* DAZ.

MOTHER: It's three-thirty in the morning. What the hell were you doing? You could have been lying dead in the gutter.

CHORUS: [*Whisper*] Utter nutter!

MOTHER: And you stink of booze. Have you been taking anything else? [DAZ *shakes head*] You don't tell me where you're going and I stay up half the night worrying. I can't help it. Even the sleeping pills didn't work tonight. What are you trying to do to me? I was sick with fear.

CHORUS: [*Whisper*] Great gear.

MOTHER: I can't cope with it any more. Don't you understand? I lost your father. I don't want to lose you.

16

She half shakes, half hugs him as Daz *slips out of her grasp and is carried offstage by* Chorus *as if to bed.*

CHORUS: Whoah! Is it the bed that's moving or the walls? Wheeeee!

They sway him round and carry him off. Lights dim before daylight appears once more.

Cast enter in character, putting school ties around necks, move stools in front of benches to form desks and take up positions. Daz *enters in school uniform, looking moody.*

TEACHER: Why are you late, Brightson? Your exam leave is only a few weeks away. This must not go on.

COL: Oh, don't go on, sir. Prince Whatsisface got married to Lady Spenceroni this weekend.

ROSY: We had to raise a toast,

MINNIE: Or ten,

ADE: To celebrate the happy coupling. And coupling is nearly the word from what I hear, eh, Daz?

MINNIE: Daz getting it on with a girl? We'll be hearing bells soon.

COL: Yes, Daz has got a big pair of bells!

ALL: [*Chanting*] For he's a jolly good fellow, for he's a jolly good fellow…

Daz *looks up and manages a smile.*

ROSY: Our dear Daz got a bit carried away

COL: To another solar system in fact.

TEACHER: I get the point. But we need to be studying what's on *this* planet, eh, Brightson? Forget fairy-tale princes and princesses. Focus. Think exams, exams, exams.

DAZ *nods and shuffles to desk.*

TEACHER: [*Exasperated*] Thank you. We are trying to learn about terminal velocity… when you are quite ready?

DAZ *is silent. Goes to his desk. He is upset but mustn't show it. Two pupils from* CHORUS *are sniffing correction fluid thinner (mimed), putting it on a handkerchief and sniffing. They look dazed.* DAZ *joins them. Freeze.*

CHORUS:

1:	School
2:	Is dull for Daz
3:	No doubt about it.
4:	After a night out on the razz.
5:	Just another woolly day:
6:	A get-off-your-face-
7	And-hope-it-all-goes-away day.
8:	What's there to learn?
9:	Families fall apart and burn,
10:	Passing exams in misery,
1:	He studies his father's history.
2:	Daz is taught that love's a lie
3:	But beneath the wasted high
4:	He's quiet
5:	Inside him a riot
6:	Of feelings, message in a bottle, corked and waiting
7:	Ignore the past and go for the dating!

All freeze. Spotlight on DAZ *who walks to end of bench and picks up* COL's *hand to use as a phone. Mimes coin push in for payphone. Sound effect, engaged tone.*

School group forms silent rugby scrum.

DAZ: The world is too busy for me, I tried to engage, wondering if the drunken laughs and lust were just a bad connection. I made the wrong pass, went head down for the dealer instead, tried to dance and drug my feelings away. Then she, Bel of the Ball, kicks me into touch. But I can't give it up this easily...

Phone starts ringing and is picked up.

BEL: [*Offstage*] Hello?

DAZ: I fumble my words,

Dropping my stutters

I'm no match for her.

All I ever know how to score

Is the stuff that will take me away,

And out of it, and evermore

She's the winner's cup,

And I'm running down the line

Anxious for just one try...

BEL: [*Offstage interrupts monologue*] So... great... see you later, then.

DAZ: [*Arms go up*] Yes! Yes! Yes!

He pushes scrum, which collapses. School group re-form in tableau. Lights dim.

BEL *enters centre stage: she is waiting for* DAZ *to turn up.* DAZ *is at the edge of the stage but* BEL *can't see him as he paces up and down, indecisive. This scene is done as a dance.* CHORUS *step forward. As they speak, words initiate movements.*

1:	Patient princess,
2:	Lady-in-waiting
3:	For the boy we guess
4:	Is not used to dating.
5:	Will he honour his pledge?
6:	She checks her wrist.
7:	He's on the edge.
8:	This loving tryst,
9:	This possible touch,
10:	Such happiness
1:	Is all too much.
2:	It's all a mess
3:	And too grown up,
4:	The prince has stood
5:	The princess up.

DAZ *looks back at* BEL *one more time and exits. She is crestfallen.*

BEL *puts tie on. School scene.* BEL *enters as pupil, along with* CHORUS *who also put on ties.*

GIRL 1:   But why him? You knew he wouldn't turn up! His only passion is powders! And I am not talking the stuff you dab on your face.

20

GIRL 2:   Off your face and up your nose! [*Girls laugh*]

BEL: [*Jumping up and going into role-playing angry
           teacher*] Thank you so much for your support. But
           you have got no idea – so, young and inexperienced,
           passionless pupils, listen and learn... I can't just give up
           now. Maybe he got the wrong place or something?

GIRL 3:   Likely. And my mother is a wombat.

GIRL 4:   She is, actually.

GIRL 3:   Shut it.

BEL: Excuse me. Well, I am excusing him, don't know why.
           But there was something that night. When he was
           really out of it, he started clinging on to me. There
           was something sad under all that bravado.

GIRL 1:   But how can you like him? He's stood you up.

BEL: I don't know that for sure. Maybe I'm just a bit older.
           And don't you see? He's been dumped on all his life.
           Forget the hard man. That's his mask – visor down,
           lance ready and you'd better not be on the receiving
           end. But the armour he wears gets a bit heavy. I had
           a chance to get under the chainmail.

GIRL 2:   Now you're talking

ALL: Phwoarrr!

BEL: Oh, why do I bother?

GIRL 1:   Go on, then.

BEL: Well, I thought I'd just go round his house, on my
           way home, see if he had forgotten and his mum was
           there – asked me in for a cup of tea and next minute,

poured it all out. No wonder she's a nervous wreck. She told me what happened, all about the lovely husband (she showed me some pictures and he looks so much like Daz), who got depressed and killed himself, leaving her with two small children and no money. The older one grew up and got smacked out of his brains and Daz is the piggy in the middle. I don't call that the happiest family in the world, do you? Then I came along and maybe it was all too much.

Girl 2: So what for the sob story? He's just like any bloke. The moment they've had you, they're on to the next conquest. They wouldn't know faithfulness if it smacked them in the gob. Knight in shining armour? Forget it.

Bel: Give me a chance. It explains everything. Yes, I sat there, all dolled up. I didn't feel like a princess, just a prat. And maybe you *are* right. But maybe not. It's not me he's stood up. It's love. Yeah, love. It's a vomit-worthy word, but some people still believe in it. He's had everything taken away from him. Why should he believe I would be any different? Fairy tales don't come true – that's the lesson life has taught him. So, he just chucked me before I could chuck him. Any other questions?

Girl 4: Yeah, what happens next?

Bel: I don't know. I wrote him a letter – as if that would

do any good. Said I knew about his past and offered to be his friend, though I want to be more than that! I'm just a gullible, good-hearted girl, you know.

Girls step back into CHORUS. *Blackout except for single spot on* BEL, *who sits down and writes a letter.*

BEL: [*Reading aloud*] I don't know if you were there or not and you're probably expecting me to tell you to sod off. But I won't and I'm not. Meet me and give it a chance. You can't carry the past like a ball and chain for ever. You know what I am talking about. This is the present. Forget about the past. See you soon? Love Bel.

DAZ *is still at the side of the stage. Lights fade on* BEL *and come up on him as he repeats her last words.*

DAZ: This is the present and forget about the past. [*He sounds worried.* BEL *moves to side of stage*] But how can I forget that day? It's still present inside, burning. I was only little, but I could tell my dad was unhappy. He didn't throw me up in the air any more and Mum was always telling me to leave him alone. Perhaps it was my fault... But at least he came back every night. Mum cuddled us a lot, saying that his work was very hard and that was why he was so tired in the evenings. But that day, a taxi came to get us from school. Mum was white-faced and the house was empty. She told me 'Daddy had a car accident and went to heaven'. I only found out the truth years

23

later. I thought heaven was like some hospital and kept asking when we could visit and when he was coming home... Mum was great, rock solid, bless her, strong for us. Now I know that her love just shrivelled up inside her and died at that moment. I don't know if she'll ever love again. That day, I didn't cry at all. I don't cry. Ever. [*Pause*] My brother was the one who went ape. He just let it all out and now it's smack that covers the cracks. I just went quiet. But the pain is still there. Dope softens it and sulphate helps me talk it away through the numbing night... And then this girl, this one-night armour-piercing bloody fling has stirred it all up. Too much hassle. Forget it, I'm out of here. This is no fun.

CHORUS *step forward.* DAZ *walks onstage, about to take a trip.* BEL *reads the letter again in background, whispered. She repeats* Love Bel *over and over at the end.*

1:	Daz is on the run.
2:	The letter
3:	Doesn't make things better
4:	But worse.
5:	Living and loving is a cruel curse.
6:	Sod the relationship
7:	Take the ultimate smiley trip.
8:	Not so fab,
9:	He swallows a tab.

9:      The crack's growing wide.

10:     There's nowhere to hide.

Chorus *whisper* hide *to* Daz *as he walks faster and faster, then begins to spin round like a dervish.*

1:      This hint of love is far too much

2:      For a boy who is out of touch.

3:      Now momentum begins to whirl [Bel *looks up and starts walking towards* Daz]

4:      Him

All: Away

4:      From this gracious girl

5:      Daz is ready to take a degree

6:      His subject? The nightmare vision of

All: LSD!

Benches lined up to make bus seats. Chorus *drag* Bel *away from* Daz. *Sound of water rushing. Loud discordant sounds to the tune of 'The wheels of the bus go round and round', chanted off-key by* Chorus.

Stage divided in two – Daz *is on the bus on the left side, which has banal, normal conversations. This is juxtaposed with the chaos of* Daz's *visions performed on the right of the stage, accompanied by music and surreal lighting. Cutting between the two should create a stark contrast. Half of* Chorus *sit with* Daz *and minimal props, e.g. handbag, Walkman. Movements and swaying on bus must be perfectly timed, with* Daz *seated in middle looking out of window.* Chorus *set the scene:*

1:      Summer night

2:      On the top deck

3:      Surfing the city streets

4:      Riding the tarmac tides

5:      Phosphor in the depths

1:      It's sparkly

2:      Looking through the glass

3:      Darkly

4:      Green leaves

5:      Brushing the windows

1:      The rhythm and flow

2:      The breath and the glow

3:      Perfect trip

4:      But then things

ALL: Slip!

Bus veers left, all lean over. Screech of brakes. Left side of stage blacks out. Bus characters freeze. CHORUS *on right side come to life with spotlight on* DAZ. *Five* CHORUS *members are lined up behind each other facing audience. Each lean to side to speak their lines, then stand upright.*

6:      Heart attack!

ALL: Flashback!

6:      Head case

7:      Case of the head

8:      Choices

9:      Voices

10:     Come on, Daz

6:      Are you ready to

7:      Die

8:      Today

9:      Are you ready

10:     Today

6:      To die

7:      Are you ready

8:      To Daz

9:      To dee

10:     Do die dooby dooby doo

DAZ *looks around, panicking. Switch back to bus, with veering movements and conversations.* DAZ *is wild eyed. Bus characters freeze.*

Lights up on right. CHORUS *become game show hosts with cheesy voices.*

6:      And our lucky loser is…

7:      Daz Brightson!

8:      Daz, the choice of voice is yours!

9:      It's up to you, Daz.

Drumroll, CHORUS *face audience.*

10:     Will he choose…

6:      Number one: the fairy-tale ending!

ALL: Ahhhhhh!

7:      Number two: you're a failure!

8:      Number three: you don't deserve this girl!

9:      Number four: jump from the building!

10:      The anticipation is intense. [*Clock ticking loudly*]

6:       What will it be?

ALL: [*As* DAZ *gets up and leaves the bus*] It's... jump the building! [*Each word is emphasised as if this is a game.* CHORUS *applauds, shouts of* Go for it Daz! Show your old man you can do it!]

CHORUS *join together into one group, move benches constantly to make spotlit shifting path and obstacles for* DAZ *as he attempts to walk along the street. Drug gang enter and see* DAZ.

JEFF: All right, Daz?

ROSY: Where have you been? We were worried.

DAZ: On a trip. To see my father.

MINNIE: But your dad's dead. You're losin' it, Daz.

DAZ: I'm fine. Going somewhere. Leave me.

ADE: Bel's been trying to get hold of you. She said you didn't turn up.

DAZ: Bel tolling. Nothing to hold on to.

COL: You're acting a bit crazy, mate! Is this a bad trip or what?

DAZ: A good journey. I must leave now. Good day to you. Go! Go!

ALL: Daz? Daz?

He pushes them away.

JEFF: Just leave him to it. The guy is tripped out. I've got some great gear back at the squat.

Gang exit. ROSY *looks back.*

ROSY: Take care, Daz.

DAZ *mimes walking up steps.*

DAZ: There are voices in my head. I will climb this multi-story, strain against the sky. I am a dangerous Icarus with no provision but feathers and wax. But my heart is melting as I fly to meet my father. We have a date. I shall tell him I miss him. Like father, like burning bloody sun. Oh well, here we are. [*He has reached the ledge, which is the front of the stage.* CHORUS *have lined up with him, all on tiptoes with* DAZ *in middle*] This is the edge. The moment between now and then. I teeter and sway. What wind will carry me? My father's footsteps are loud in my ears. Have courage. My shoulders itch. I will be an angel…

ALL: Now!

Mood takes a surreal change – into Hollywood-style musical piece, using words as rhythm – top hats, canes, finger-clicking, inventive use of benches and stools and posh Noel Coward voices. DAZ *is the centre of this dance. The cheerful style of presentation should cut across the subject matter to create a dark skit. Puns need to be heavily emphasised and the pace sufficiently measured to get the bleak jokes. Dance is synchronised.*

1:      Some say it's a sin

2:      To do yourself in

3:      Glamorous pop stars

4:      Cease their singing

5:      With a way out exit,

6:      Really swinging,

7:      For teenage angst

        [*Melodramatic back of hand on forehead*]

        the perfect antic,

ALL: It's so impossibly romantic.

        [*All sigh as if in love, with hand on heart*]

5:      If you feel cut up,

6:      Your head's in a twist,

        [*Hands on head, melodramatic*]

7:      And it's all in vein, [*Tap with cane*]

8:      You need a little wrist.

9:      If friends are bored by your sensitive sighing

        [*Sigh and tut*]

10:     Shock them with an end electrifying!

        [*Put hands up and shake*]

1:      How to get over having the hump?

        [*Hands on hips*]

2:      Choose a ten-storey car park.

ALL: Then jump!

CHORUS *raise left feet up as if about to step over edge, and bring down in unison with big bang. Cast freeze. Blackout.* DAZ *exits.*

Lights up. Chorus *re-arrange benches for classroom, then move back.*

TEACHER: Terminal velocity. Now, when two stones of different weight and mass are both dropped, which reaches the ground first?

ADE: That's easy, sir – both land at the same time.

MINNIE: Well done, it's creepy-Ade, the teacher's pet drink!

COL: [*Slurping noise*] Sucking up!

DAZ: [*Enters, shuffling towards chair mumbling under his breath*] Like father, like son.

TEACHER: Are you all right, Daz?

COL: I don't think he is, sir! Hey, what happened last night? You were really out of it.

MINNIE: Yeah, glad to see you back in the land of the living.

ROSY: For a second we thought that you might have…

TEACHER: Fallen. Two stones. Which one hits the ground first?

DAZ *slumps to the ground.*

ROSY: Hey! Daz!

Gang back away, scared. He comes to, starts flailing on floor. CHORUS *close in on* DAZ *gently, cradling him.*

DAZ: [*Shouting*] Mummy, I want my mummy, I want my mummy.

Class look shocked. Improvise comments: What the hell's going on? Christ, he's lost it! *etc.*

TEACHER: Um. Er. I think you'd better all leave now. I'll… er… get the Head. I think Daz needs to… to… to go home. Come along now. [*Gang exit.* MOTHER *enters*]

MOTHER: [*To* CHORUS] Give him to me now. [CHORUS *hand* DAZ *over and move back*] When I first met my husband, it was electric. So tall, almost gawky, but handsome, yes, he was. Didn't matter that his ears were big. He heard me, that's what counts. I just knew. That's the truth. There's an old picture of us going out to a Hawaiian fancy dress party. Me, young and pretty in a hula skirt. Him in that naff shirt, with a grin on his face that still gets me every time I look. That's the time I keep him in. My prince. We were the happy-ever-after couple. [*Pause*] After… after the two delightful boys… Actually Daz was a bit of a screamer from the word go. Once screamed for two weeks non-stop. They gave him barbiturates to calm him down. A six-year-old drug addict. [*Laughs to herself*] But that was after. After the two wonderful boys and business struggling and my husband never talking about his feelings. He just sat there night after night, worrying about work and how he would look after us if the company went down. I said I'd love him whatever, but he felt like a failure as a man and just let it all pile up inside him and the doctors gave him pills and the depression grew deep and the distance between us got wider and I knew that day, yes, I knew… [*Pause*] He wanted to take us with him, and I got angry, angrier than I've ever been. I told him, 'Do what you want with your life, but leave us

32

out of it.' I was so scared, I even kept the kitchen knife handy in case he tried to take our boys away. [CHORUS *sit down in semi circle to listen to the story*] There was a place in the woods, out of town. His den, he called it. Went there to get away from it all sometimes. And I knew, that morning. It was a cold October day, damp, bed empty, ring his secretary, not there, drive too bloody fast, run through the trees… and he's there, my beautiful boy, his baby-blue eyes wide, wide… I worked it out. He had climbed the pylon and jumped straight on to the wire. [DAZ *opens his eyes*] And his fists, still clenched, black from the voltage and the cable, trying to grasp at something and holding, holding on… I rocked him then, rocked my husband in my arms [*Rocking* DAZ] and now I'm rocking you, my son. [*Singing*] You are my sunshine, my only sunshine…

MOTHER *sobs, holding* DAZ, *stroking his head. Lights fade.*

ACT 2

CHORUS *commentate.* DAZ *wanders around as if in a daze, holding his mother's hand.*

1:      The next morning,

2:      The world has washed from his mind.

3:      Poor Daz can't find

4:      The bottle to do himself in.

5:      His mind's in a spin

6:      This trip won't stop

7:      He leaves his mates

8:      Hallucinates.

9:      Mother holds his screwed-up hand.

10:     What doctor could ever understand?

DAZ *shakes off his mother's hand and runs, chasing an imaginary piece of rubbish.*

1:      Mother plucks at the sudden grey of her hair.
        Time flies.

MOTHER: There, there [*Grabs his hand*],

2:      Leads him to the psychiatrist's lair

CHORUS *bow like courtiers as* DAZ *and his mother sweep past.*
CHORUS *form doors that swing inwards.* DAZ *and* MOTHER *stop in front.*

DAZ: I have come to the castle gates. They shall open
        before me. [*He puts his hands up and doors swing
        open*] Cool corridors await me, and bustling courtiers,
        pretending to ignore this prince.

CHORUS *breaks up and rush around becoming doctors and nurses in hospital.* MOTHER *drags* DAZ *up to an official-looking woman.*

1:          Your appointment is at 10.30. Please take a seat.

DAZ: I shall be appointed. [*Sits down on bench with* MOTHER] I am seated in the ante-room, before my audience with the king. Ah...! But I forget. My mind is not what it was. Forgive me. The king is dead. Yes, dead. That is right. Wounded mortally in the forest.

MOTHER: [*Stroking his hand*] Yes.

1:          Mrs Brightson! Mrs Brightson! [*Receptionist indicates direction*] Dr Geoff will see you now. First left, then right.

They walk down a corridor formed by the CHORUS' *arms. Door opens,* DOCTOR *at bench scribbling notes.* CHORUS *all mirror* DOCTOR'*s movements from back.* DAZ *and* MOTHER *sit.*

DAZ: [*Whispering to audience*] The king's counsel! I must have his word. Prince Brightson must have and heed and hold, for his father the king is dead.

DOCTOR: [*Scribbling*] And how long have these symptoms been presenting themselves?

MOTHER: Seven days. He's not himself. He cries like a baby and gets so scared. [*Pause*] But, at other times, he seems totally at peace.

DOCTOR: This anxiety level can occur in patients, though he is very young.

MOTHER: But what is it? Is he schizophrenic?

DOCTOR: No, this is fairly mild. If you are desperate for a label, then 'adolescent identity crisis' would be closer to a diagnosis. The drugs he has been taking won't have helped.

MOTHER: But he only smokes a bit of cannabis. He told me himself. He's never taken heroin like his brother.

DOCTOR: I'm afraid I must be blunt. This is more than the occasional joint, more even than cannabis paranoia, Mrs Brightson. He has certainly been taking hallucinogens very recently. It is possible he has succumbed to an extended LSD flashback – what young people call 'a bad trip' – which hasn't yet stopped. It may even be a form of amphetamine psychosis. We can admit him immediately and start him off on 100 milligrams of largactil and some temazepam to help him sleep.

MOTHER: Sleep. I haven't slept since they brought him home from school. Yesterday, he asked me to put away all the knives in the house. He told me about the car park and the voices telling him to jump. Thank God he had the courage not to... [*Distracted*] My husband was such a lovely man...

DOCTOR: Mrs Brightson?

MOTHER: Yes, yes.

DAZ: I worship her from afar. It is courtly love*. You must understand. The Lady Bel awaits my presence. [*Turns*

* Stylised idolisation of a female, originating from Medieval times.

to MOTHER] Who are you?

MOTHER *kisses him goodbye, shakes hand sadly with* DOCTOR *and both exit.* DAZ *stays seated.* CHORUS *gather.*

1:       He is so confused.

2:       Thinks he's in a castle.

3:       Now he is feverish.

4:       His mother has left him in good hands.

5:       Come, ladies-in-waiting.

DAZ *shakes all over as nurses tend to him.*

6:       Come to him, and apply soothing ointments.

7:       This prince has been in battle.

8:       Bathe his wounds.

9:       Reassure him that he shall see his princess again.

10:     They have stripped him and he is naked as the newborn.

1:       Such a white, angelic child.

2:       Apply to him herbs.

3:       Help him sleep.

Lights dim, chant of Sleep! Sleep! Sleep! *as he is being led towards a bed, improvised from benches and a pair of hands as a pillow. He tosses and turns.*

4:       How he battles quieter [*Stroking his head*]

5:       With the dark dragon.

6:       Soils himself,

3:       Getting rid of all that crap inside.

7:       Life is crappy sometimes!

9:      Come dawn, bring light and good counsel.

10:     Words are swords that will save the day.

1:      As if...

CHORUS *move benches into circle and move back. Lights up,* DAZ *sits up, psychiatric unit characters enter to sit round for group therapy.*

DOCTOR: Welcome, Daz. This is our therapy group. Now, perhaps you'd like to begin and tell us what's going on for you today?

DAZ: The king is dead. I killed him.

DOCTOR: I see. How does this make you feel?

DAZ: [*Confused*] What does the privy council make of it?

ROSE: It was the battle that took the king, not your brave self.

DOCTOR: Please don't play Daz's games, Nurse Rose.

Another patient is constantly shuffling about, looking at the window.

DOCTOR: The window is barred, Bella. You'd have to be thin as a leaf to slip through.

AMEENA: We have all slipped through the net.

DOCTOR: Perhaps the group would like to introduce themselves.

CHORUS *step forward and mime characters' stories.*

COLIN: I am Colin, found wandering,
          No shoes, no shirt, no coat for the cold,
          Like a child, I was brought to the ward,
          Mugged of all my memory,

A scabbard without a sword.

AMEENA: I am Ameena, pushed and pushed by my parents,
Until the sickening start
Of a bawling beautiful madness
And voices in the house of my heart.

AIDEN: I am Aiden, the waiter, my mind a scrambled dish,
Dropped on depression's floor, my only simple wish
To clear the hurt in my head,
They gave me ECT, electrified my dread
To make the darkness flee.

AMEENA: That's Bella, always threatening like our English
weather as she makes a clouded shuffle round the
room. The nurses never take her seriously. They keep
saying 'Go on then, attention seeking'. One day…
[*Characters freeze.* CHORUS *circle*]

7: This is Daz's new gang.

8: All pretty stoned.

9: Largactil, temazepam, valium, and that wakey-wakey
ECT.

10: Shocking really.

1: Shake some sense into them.

2: The word on the ward is:

3: Let's escape to the pub!

DOCTOR: The session is done for the day. This is your time now,
make the best of it.

DOCTOR *and* NURSE *exit.*

AMEENA: Thirsty work, this therapy stuff. Fancy a drink, folks?

COLIN: At least I can remember the taste of lager!

AIDEN: How about you, Daz?

DAZ: [*Nods his head*] We shall mix with the common
           people outside the gates of the castle. I shall be
           disguised and hope that none fall like fools to their
           knees in front of me. But we are the fools. Wounded,
           shuffling knights. The battle has not done us good.
           We must wear brave faces.

*Hospital group jostles in queue for drinks, improvise orders,
mime going outside to sit on benches.* CHORUS *form rest of pub
scene, with hubbub in the background as following characters
speak.*

DAZ: My words are slower now. The herbs they give have
           slurred my speech. But outside the castle…

AMEENA: There are trees

COLIN: Summer flowers in baskets

AIDEN: Streets like shining moats

AMEENA: The bustle of the rush hour

COLIN: Market fair.

Hubbub dies down.

AMEENA: There are voices inside my head.

DAZ: Me too!

COLIN: I have mislaid my memory.

DAZ: I also.

AIDEN: I am the waiter at the turning table, waiting to be
           well.

DAZ: I too am waiting, for my father.

AIDEN: Is he coming to get you?

DAZ: He will send an army of shadows!

COLIN: What does he look like?

DAZ: I do not remember so well, except his rough cheeks when he held me. He used to throw me up in the air, so high I could almost fly. But he fought in a far country and has not returned yet. I went to join him, but could not find the way.

AMEENA: You miss him like mad?

DAZ: Mad, yes. Mad with grief, mad at losing my way.

AMEENA: Hey!

BELLADONNA *wanders in road.* CHORUS *form speeding cars.*

AMEENA: Bella, come back, you crazy cow.

DAZ: She is courting death, hoping the horses run her down. I shall go to her. [DAZ *steps out into 'traffic' which screeches to a halt and parts. He leads Bella back to bench*] My lady, drink this. [*Lifts drink to her lips*] The horse of night will gallop on. I too have ridden it, towards the groves of my father. Too far, and there is no turning back. Now, soft, soft. [*He strokes her hair*] There is also the matter of a princess.

AMEENA: We're all ears.

DAZ: She helped me forget about my father for a while. Such a night in our bedchamber.

AIDEN: I can't wait to hear what happens next. Go on, titillate the loonies!

DAZ: Nothing. She is gone.

AMEENA: Oh well, plenty more fish in the sea. Oh forget it, sod the bloody fish. Life is crap.

COLIN: You'll remember love one day. I hope I do.

AIDEN: Just wait it out. That's what I do. Come on Daz, let's get back.

All move across stage back to psychiatric unit. Hospital characters melt away.

BEL *enters, with gang behind.*

BEL: Daz? Daz? [*She goes up and kisses him on the lips. He turns away*]

JEFF: We heard you were in a loony bin.

ROSY: Jeff!

DAZ: Daz not so bright now. Turned out. Switched off. Wounded.

MINNIE: This place gives me the spooks.

COL: Not exactly a palace is it?

ADE: Love the slight scent of stale urine.

BEL: Daz, are you all right? Your mum told me. I can't believe it. I can almost forgive you not turning up for our date, git face. What's happened?

DAZ: Happened? Everything. The potion I took was too strong. I tried to join my father but he didn't want me. So I carried on breathing. I met this princess one night. She was too beautiful and bright. I must destroy her before she strips off my armour.

BEL *shrinks away.*

JEFF: Hey, back off, space cadet! This girl is just trying to help.

ROSY: I think he's still tripping. Comedown city or what?

BEL: Daz, listen. I talked to your mum. She told me everything. I know about your dad. Pushing me away won't help.

DAZ: He is in a far country. He was injured. He shall return.

BEL: No, he won't, Daz. You're running away.

DAZ: I'm scared now.

BEL: [*Holds him*] You're shaking.

DAZ: I am not well. I seek the king's counsel.

JEFF: Well, we can't have you hanging out with those weirdos.

COL: Yeah, we are a better class of nutters.

ADE: [*Whispers in his ear, so that* BEL *can't hear*] You need some puff to calm you down, mate.

DAZ: My fellow knights, we have been wounded by the dreadful drug-on.

MINNIE: Drugon? Dragon? What are you on about Daz? In fact, what are you on, Daz?

DAZ: I'm confused.

ROSY: [*Hugs him*] I'm not surprised, darling. You'll be OK.

MINNIE: Let's get this psycho out of Sicko Street.

COL: You shouldn't be in here. We'll smuggle you out!

BEL: Do you think this is a good idea?

ALL: Yes!

COL: Lighten up, Bel.

ADE: [*Produces wig*] Ear wig go, ear wig go, ear wig go!

DAZ: Forsooth. A cunning disguise. I surrender to this
         worthy band.

They smuggle him out of imaginary gates.

JEFF: Party tonight! Are you coming, Bel?

BEL: No, I don't feel well. Look. He's not supposed to mix
         his medication with drink or anything, right? It could
         be dangerous.

JEFF: Don't worry. We'll look after him.

BEL: Your 'looking after him' got him in here in the first
         place, Jeff. [*To* DAZ] Watch yourself tonight. Please.
         [*She touches him on shoulder, and exits*]

ROSY: Just like old times. You'll be fine.

MINNIE: Just keep it under control.

DAZ: Bring me wine and give me potions to calm me.

JEFF: All in good time mate, all in good time.

*They walk round the stage, open an imaginary door, music
blasts out. A party is taking place including* CHORUS. *Some
characters are dancing, some wasted.* JEFF *and* DAZ *sit. As they
speak, dancers freeze.*

JEFF: Only the best stuff for you, mate.

DAZ: You have brought me moonlight.

JEFF: That's it, well mushroom punch actually. Gives a good
         punch too. [*They giggle*] A couple of lines?

DAZ: I gallop on the white horse. The wind is jealous. The king is near.

ROSY: Elvis has returned!

ADE: Ever thought of taking up poetry, mate?

MINNIE: This bard is off his bonce!

DAZ: I am poisoned. Hush. I have trusted my kinsmen too
             much. I must, I must...

DAZ *lurches up, pushes them out of way, and staggers from
party which dissolves.* CHORUS *now line edges of stage with
arms out.* DAZ *lurches from one to another while* CHORUS
whispers It's all in your mind *and* Do you mind? *and* Mind the
gap! *He collapses as whispers get louder.*

1:           And in the night, he is found and returned.

CHORUS *carry* DAZ *gently on to a bench.*

2:           Back to the ward

3:           Filled with words

4:           Like blackbirds

6:           Flying

7:           Comedown

8:           Come dawn.

ALL: Crash!

He screams. NURSE ROSE *comes running, dressed now in fairy
godmother outfit with a wand. This is part of* DAZ's
hallucination. She soothes his face. CHORUS *echo some of* NURSE's
words.

NURSE: Liquor just makes you sicker, dear Daz.

CHORUS: [*Whisper*] Sicker, sicker, sicker.

NURSE: Oh, boy. What have you learned from your big night

out? Take that brick and just keep hittin' yourself.
That brick won't build nothin'.

DAZ: [*Moaning*] But the king, the king… I must reach the king.

CHORUS: [*Whisper*] The king is dead, dead, dead.

NURSE: You forget about him, honey. He did you no good. Why, a father that ran out on you, leaving two beautiful boys and that darlin' wife. You don't want to go with him. He was the one that got really wasted.

DAZ: It's all I know.

NURSE: And all I know is, that just ain't the way. It ain't on the cards for you. [*She pulls out pack of cards, flourishes her wand over it*] Now, I know they got you pills and therapy and all sorts here. But I got my own healing for you. [*She shuffles*] The cards say you've been a bad boy – Jack of the all-night clubs running away.

CHORUS: Stay, stay, stay.

NURSE: That's your past. Pass it by. Here's your future. Open your eyes.

CHORUS: No more highs! Highs. Highs…

NURSE: Here, I told you. Queen of Hearts, my love. It tells me about some girl who keeps waiting. That's your trump card. Ah, and the hanged man. Surprise, surprise. Here is the man who hangs up the phone, stays alone, breaks dates. You've got some saying sorry to do.

DAZ: I treated her like my father treated me. My wound is mortal, I cannot carry the kingdom. I am gone.

CHORUS: Gone, gone, gone.

NURSE: [*Shaking him*] You *can*, boy. Grow a bit. Get off the pity pot. It's not so hard. This here's no palace. It's a dungeon. Here we get put away, all the edges of society, the bits that don't fit. But who wants to fit? Remember, in the fairy tale, it's always the outsider who comes and sets things right. I'm not saying that your life can be happy ever after. Relationships, even those of princes and princesses, screw up sometimes. Yeah, you are wounded, but it's part of you, makes you what you are. One day, you'll see it's a gift, boy, your ace of coming-up spades – the cards give you hope.

CHORUS: Hope, hope, not dope.

NURSE: It takes time. Just open the door, and walk. I'll be with you.

NURSE *exits.*

Lights up for next day. DAZ *is holding his head in his arms.*

AMEENA: Hey, heard you had a bad night.

DAZ: To put it mildly, my lady.

AMEENA: Isn't it time you dropped all this 'My lady this', 'Forsooth that' crap?

DAZ: Yeah. But the castle's strong, under siege. I must keep within the walls.

AMEENA: Daz?

DAZ: All right. I am here actually. [*Sighs*] Not a good idea mixing the pills they give you with drink and all those party drugs.

AMEENA: What they inject me with is bad enough. Helps with the nightmares though... sometimes.

DAZ: It was a nightmare. I just wanted it to be like the old days. The fairy tale. Out with your mates, in a warm room somewhere, anywhere... good music, great spliffs, a couple of lines, a bit of a laugh. But last night, it just didn't work any more. No matter how much I took, it did nothing except make me more confused. And they were all so glad to see me... or seemed to be.

AMEENA: Fair-weather friends. Before I broke down at university, I had loads of those. My family, dead keen, pushing me all the while. But when the pressure got too much... pouf! And the moment I was in here for my first time, they all vanished like bloody rabbits in a hat. Who wants to hang out with a sicko?

DAZ: I was a bit of a novelty item. The breakdown boy, one girl called me. Bel couldn't hack it, didn't even come to the party. I really let her down. [*Pauses*] Hey, but I'm just talking about me. Did you have a boyfriend?

AMEENA: Yeah. I wasn't always a dribbling hag. He was with

me the night I started screaming and screaming and screaming. Can't blame him really for a sharp exit. Nobody understood. Mental illness. It's like having 'weirdo' tattooed on your forehead. My family never talk about me now. They treat me like it never happened and their visits get rarer.

DAZ: The only reason my mates came was to take me to a party from which I nearly didn't come back. Nurse Rose was brilliant. I don't remember half of what she said, but it seemed to be a kind of wake-up call. I want to get better.

AMEENA: You're in with a chance. I've got a condition and all they can do is treat it. But my life does seem more real these days. [*Looks at watch*] Oh, joy. Therapy with Doctor Geoff. Come on, Daz. If you can talk to him like you talk to me, you might even be able to convince them you're no longer a nutter.

DAZ: I don't know. It's quite safe here. I don't think I'll leave just yet.

CHORUS *use vocal tick-tock rhythm and movements with appropriate lighting to indicate passing of days. There are several repeated mimed therapy groups where* DAZ *appears to become successively more animated. Music creates atmosphere. Time-passing scene ends with all exiting, putting benches to side, except* DAZ.

Enter COL *and* MINNIE *and* ADE.

COL: Wotcha.

MINNIE: Sorry, haven't been round for a few weeks. You know how it is.

DAZ: Yeah.

ADE: That party though. Wow. You were really going for it there.

DAZ: Mmmm…

ADE: And then you just vanished. Must have been some trip.

MINNIE: There's a good one on tonight. Do you wanna come?

DAZ: Don't think so.

COL: Why not?

DAZ: Have a guess.

MINNIE: You're not doing your hair tonight, are you, Daz? Come on, don't be busy. They've got to let you out once in a while.

DAZ: Is Bel all right?

COL: She was a bit freaked out by you. You were way out of it.

DAZ: I'll have to ring her. Let her know I'm sorting things out, will you Col?

ADE: Hey, you've dropped all that find-me-the-holy-grail stuff.

MINNIE: I quite liked that. Nice to be called a lady. Entertaining.

DAZ: I found it.

COL: What? Found what?

DAZ: Never mind. The point is, I'm not coming out tonight.
           Thanks for coming.

MINNIE: That's not like you, Daz.

DAZ: What am I like, Minnie? Daz. Good-for-a-laugh-
           especially-when-he's-got-gear Daz. Space-cadet-
           orbiting-off-his-trolley Daz? Look, I know you lot
           care, but your idea of helping me out is Get-him-out-
           of-it-Get-it-down-him-Daz. I can't do that any more.

MINNIE: You're not being a party pooper, are you?

DAZ: Yeah. I am. Look, send my love to the gang and all
           that. I've got to go to my group. I'm coming out
           soon, starting over. Be seeing you.

ADE: Well…

MINNIE *gives him a kiss and they exit awkwardly.* DAZ *gets up
unsteadily,* CHORUS *use tick-tock rhythm and movements.* DAZ
*mimes passing through days and nights, with lots of him
talking in mimed therapy groups. Lighting also indicates
passage of time.* NURSE *finally leads him as others enter for
group therapy.* CHORUS *arrange benches, exit.*

DOCTOR: Please take your seats. I have some sad news for you.
           As you know, this is a voluntary unit, not a locked
           ward. We can help, but cannot force help… Last
           night, Bella managed to find the fire escape. I am so
           sorry.

Silence.

DAZ: Sorry? Sorry? You bloody encouraged her. So much for counsel.

DOCTOR: It is good to hear you sounding vaguely normal again, Mr Brightson. It sounds like the bad trip you had is finally wearing off. But isn't this response more to do with your father?

DAZ: The king is dead… but hang on. I'm alive and glad I didn't do myself in. And Bella was just a hassle to you. I heard you tell her the other day, 'Go on then!' Anything to stop her pestering you with her wild eyes. You should be ashamed of yourself.

AMEENA: Rock on, Daz!

DOCTOR: Well… she kept threatening. We thought it was just drama.

NURSE: Great drama, Doctor Geoff.

DOCTOR: For God's sake, we do our best. How could we know she would tip over the edge? I'm not a total unfeeling monster. But, now you have cast me in the role of the devilish dragon Doctor. Can we please move on, Nurse Rose?

NURSE: Yes, well… Colin and I have done a lot of work on recovering his past, the librarian in the army records office was very helpful and once we found his regiment, the amnesia started to clear.

COLIN: Mugged in Hyde Park, everything dark. Glimmers. Shimmers.

NURSE: We lived on cups of tea.

COLIN: Piercing memory. A child calling my name.

NURSE: John, not Colin… and a house, and a family frantic with worry.

COLIN: And a phone number. It rings like hallelujah bells.

NURSE: This bit of lost property soon returns to his rightful owner!

DAZ: Lost and found.

NURSE: Your wife's coming this afternoon. You're all packed up and ready to go.

COLIN: Thank you. Thank you. Thank you. [*He waves at someone offstage and exits*]

DOCTOR: And Ameena?

AMEENA: The screams in my head last night, like owls. Awful. But Nurse came and the injection calmed me.

NURSE: We had to hold her down. She was thrashing like a wild thing.

DAZ: [*To* AMEENA] I think my demons should meet yours sometime. Sounds like they'd get on well. Cheers, Ameena. Hang in there. I'll come and visit, hey?

AMEENA *laughs sadly, as* DAZ *holds her hand. She exits.*

AIDEN: They took me into a room and applied electrodes to my head. ECT. Volts. Electricity. Sometimes it jolts me awake. Knocks the depression for six.

DOCTOR: The treatment seems to have worked… again. I gather your employers are standing by you.

AIDEN: It's like everything is suddenly blocked out. I don't feel bad. Just numb. Must be what the dead feel.

DAZ: The dead feel nothing, Aiden. They just pass their hurt on to the living.

AIDEN: Totally numb. Just nothing. I can function. I must go and get on now. [*He rises and exits, shuffling*]

DOCTOR: And that leaves Mr Brightson. The psychosis seems to be just a symptom of the drugs, with a lot of emotions tucked away underneath. I do hope you stop taking them, young man, and let go of your dreadful past. Your mind might not cope with an episode like this again. I know I might appear a cold fish, but believe it or not, I am glad to see you better.

NURSE: He's been hard work, this one.

DAZ: Yeah, it is hard work being loopy. It was a really bad comedown, but now I'm coming up for air. It's funny to hear my own voice talking, almost normal.

DOCTOR: Good. We can reduce your dosage, and you should be able to leave shortly.

NURSE: But no more nightly excursions, right?

DAZ: I think I'm done with all that. It was no honeymoon out there.

DOCTOR *exits.* NURSE *holds* DAZ's *hand and lets go.* DAZ *is alone.* CHORUS *enter, mime as they speak.*

1:    Trust us

2:    He's nearly there

3:    Just needs to make a call

BEL: [*On side of stage, mimes picking up phone*] Daz? Yeah?

4:	Says with all his heart, he's sorry,
5:	He put her through a maddening worry.
6:	And is it too late?
Daz:	To ask for a date? I'll turn up this time, Bel!
Bel:	Well, are you being straight with me?
7:	He is straight. The drugs are history.
Daz:	Yeah. I'm leaving tomorrow. Doctor reckons I'm in with a chance.
8:	And does he get the last dance?
Bel:	Maybe. We'll have to see. [*Puts phone down,* Bel *joins* Chorus. Daz *smiles*]
1:	Without the drugs he felt naked and raw,
2:	Unsure of winning his personal war.
3:	But he never went back, could finally see,
4:	That getting clean was victory.
5:	When he was barking, out of his tree
6:	Friends and future were a fantasy.
7:	Easier to fly on feather-white coke,
8:	And laugh at life's great big bloody joke.
9:	So off his head, nearly lost the thread.
10:	Friends succeeded, wound up dead.
1:	Now, he takes a toke of life. A puff
2:	Of late-night love is more than enough.
3:	Jacked up with hope for the days ahead
4:	He'll chase the dragon of his dreams, instead.

The End

PLAYS WITH ATTITUDE

REHEARSAL IDEAS
Exercises and ways in

1 The Chorus lines are divided for ten performers in the text. However, any sized group can be used to perform these sections. What is important is that the Chorus group as a whole maintains a collective focus and that individuals listen to each other and respond attentively.

a) Working with a common focus: as a group, play the concentration game 'billiard balls'. Mark out a large square on the floor. Everyone stands around the four sides. A leader calls out 'start' and 'stop'. On 'start', everyone moves forward in a straight line. If you're about to collide, both individuals stop, step to their left, then continue. At the edges, each person turns and moves across the square again (like a billiard ball bouncing off the cushion). Everyone stops simultaneously when commanded. After a while, the leader ceases calling instructions and the group must start and stop the motion by itself. At first, it may be obvious that individuals are controlling the movement. However, after a while, it should seem as though the group has developed its own consciousness and rhythm. The silent movement of this exercise is also visually powerful in effect.

b) Listening and responding: play 'storyround'. Sit in a circle. Each person contributes a sentence each to a story. There must be a narrative thread which makes sense and each person needs to pick up the story quickly and seamlessly. Try it with one word each.

2 On p16, the Chorus are required to move together as though they are one entity. Perform the 'one body' exercise. Join together to represent the shape and moving parts of a large animal or machine.

3 Those in the Chorus work together very closely. There must be a strong feeling of trust within the group. The person playing Daz also needs to have complete physical trust in the Chorus group as they carry him on p17, cradle him on p31 and carry, raise and lower him on p45. There are many appropriate trust games, such as:

a) Trust circle: Group stand shoulder to shoulder in a tight circle with hands raised, palms vertical. One person in the centre closes their eyes and falls gently backwards. They are caught by the waiting hands and gently pushed in another direction. The person in the middle should keep their feet on the same spot and sway and fall with a relaxed body.

b) Blindfold walk: One person is blindfolded. Two people gently steer him/her around and let him/her touch things. The person being steered should feel completely secure in trusting they will not bump into anything.

c) Baby carrier: A group of six or more lift and carry another person around the room. Experiment with raising and lowering gently.

4 The Chorus perform synchronised movements as though on a bus on pp15/16 and pp25-27. Play follow-my-leader, moving around the room. Then play it seated, with the leader seated in front. Move the leader to one end of the seated line. Create a sequence of movements which can be repeated.

Development of character

1 Choose a character. Experiment with becoming that character physically. Without speaking, enact how your character sits, walks, dresses to go out, eats, reads a book or magazine and enters a room. Try doing these actions first as yourself, then in role and comment on the differences.

2   Prepare relevant questions with which to 'hotseat' individual characters. Hotseating is where a performer answers questions in the role as a chosen character. It is important when being hotseated not to just answer verbally in the way your character would, but to think about body language and how much that communicates to an audience. Consider also how much your character uses eye contact and how much your posture gives away about how you (in role) are really feeling.

3   Write and perform a monologue in role as one of Daz's friends, about your response to visiting him at the unit.

4   In the psychiatric unit, the character of Belladonna appears but never speaks. Develop this character physically through her movements, posture, facial expression and mannerisms. Look carefully at the scenes she appears in and decide what she is doing. Play these scenes with her voicing her inner thoughts out loud. Replay them thinking her inner monologue.

5   Doctor Geoff is a high status character. Perform his lines while concentrating on how he physically demonstrates his status through eye-contact, seated posture and mannerisms.

Performing the text

1 Consider the monologues by Daz, Bel and Mum. Experiment performing them with different positioning in the stage space and evaluate the effect. Work out where your attention is focused for each stage of the monologue.

2 In groups of different sizes, take sections of the Chorus lines and try different ways of chopping up and allocating the text. Evaluate the range of possible effects.

3 The Chorus sections are intended to be carefully choreographed to create a striking visual and aural effect. The chorus is also used to focus the characters' actions on stage. Grouping and positioning therefore needs careful consideration. Experiment with creating interesting stage pictures by working on a sequence of linked tableaux (freeze-frames) for particular sections, e.g. p8, p11 and pp37/38.

PLAYS WITH ATTITUDE

ABOUT THE AUTHORS

Andrew Fusek Peters is an author, performer and playwright with many years' experience in education. His plays include *The Wild* – a promenade play with a cast of a hundred teenagers. His TV credits include BBC1's *Wham Bam Strawberry Jam*, *Carlton Country*, *Heart of the Country* and *Mark Owen's Celebrity Scooters*.
Find out more at www.tallpoet.com

Polly Peters is a drama teacher, youth and community theatre director and writer. Her published plays include *Czech Tales* and *The Mullah Nasrudin*.

Andrew Fusek Peters and Polly Peters are the original 'been there, done that' writers. Their plays grab themes such as peer pressure, relationships, bullying, drinking and drugs and don't let go until they're finished.
Together, they have written thirty plays, anthologies, and storybooks, including the bestselling, critically acclaimed teenage collection for Hodder Wayland
– *Poems with Attitude*:

'… bursting with the raw emotion and hormone-fuelled experimentation of youth … It is rare and welcome to find a collection that speaks so directly to teenagers'
– *The Guardian*

'I cannot emphasise how much every school needs this'
– *The School Librarian*.

'Gems that make you think about real issues'
– *Daily Telegraph*

ABOUT THE CONSULTANT

Pauline Sidey Lisowska has taught English and Drama in schools and colleges throughout the UK. An author, editor and theatre director, she has also worked as a consultant for the BBC. She is currently producing a film and directing poetry shows in London's West End.

Plays with Attitude

*If you've enjoyed 'Dragon Chaser',
try these other titles in the series:*

Angelcake

'In just one moment, his whole life changed, and mine did too. He knew the risks, but then again we all do. Who ever thinks it will happen to them?' This play charts a young man's agonizing journey through AIDS, told through the eyes of his sister.

Suitable for Key Stage 4 and above

Much Ado About Clubbing

A normal Saturday night out turns into a series of hysterical cheesy chat-ups, Olympic tongue-training sessions and embarrassing drunken moments, when a group of wannabe Casanovas and flighty flirts hit the town for some serious action.

Suitable for Key Stage 3/4

Twisted

Only one thing is certain: a girl is in a coma. How she got there and what actually happened is a mystery. As the plot thickens, expect the unexpected. Who is the real victim here?

Suitable for Key Stage 3/4

You can buy all these books from your local bookseller, or order them direct from the publisher. For more information about *Plays with Attitude*, write to: *The Sales Department, Hodder Children's Books, a division of Hodder Headline Limited, 338 Euston Road, London, NW1 3BH.*